Melanie Ma
Book

MW01609862

Legendary Art Pop and Famous Electro Millennial Star, Beautiful Singer and Prodigy Artist Inspired Adult Coloring Book

Lindsey Franklin

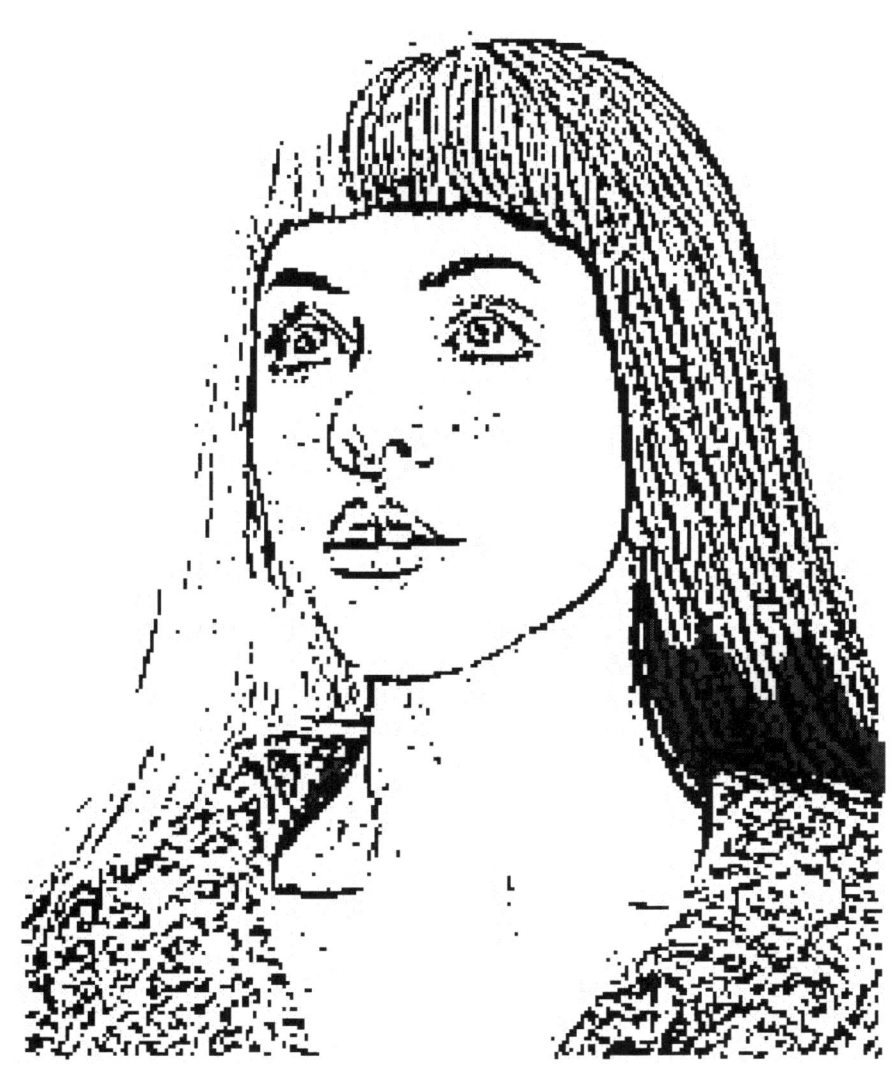

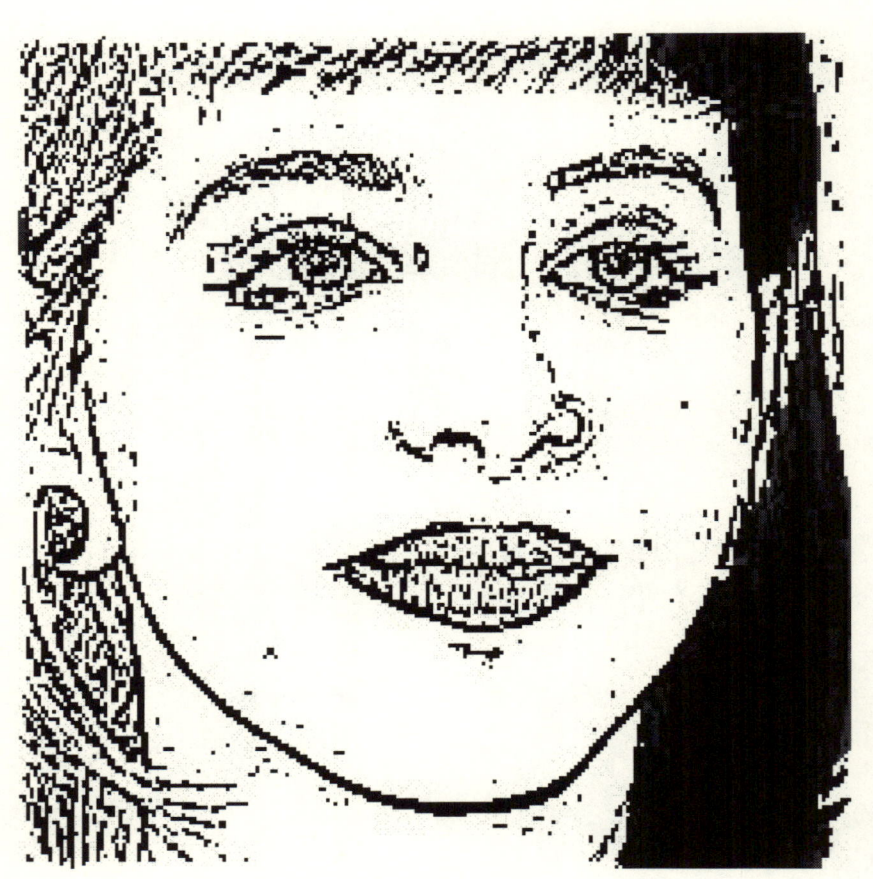

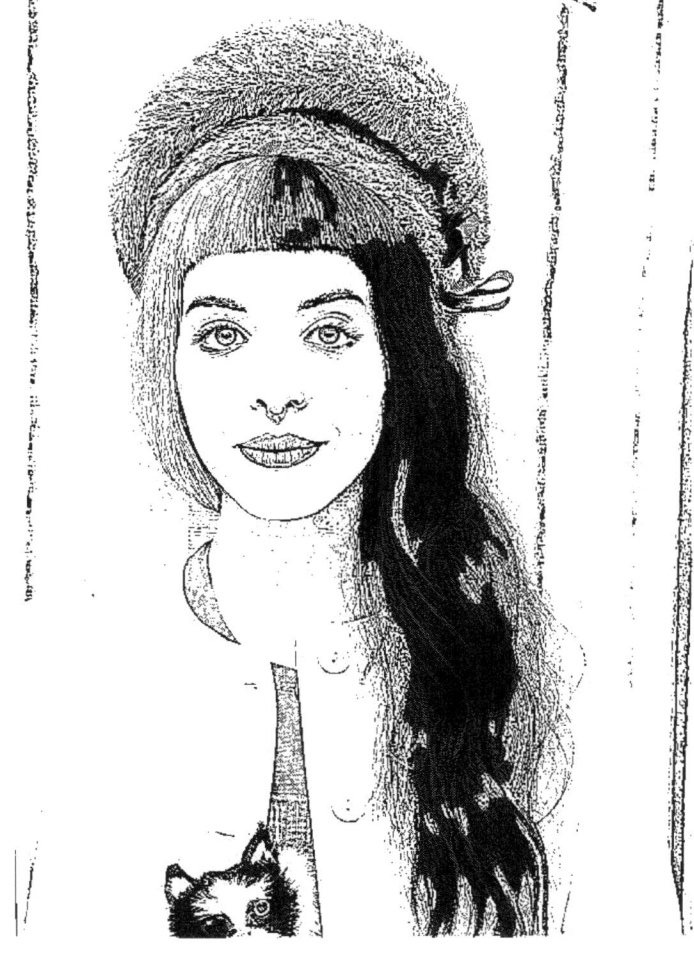

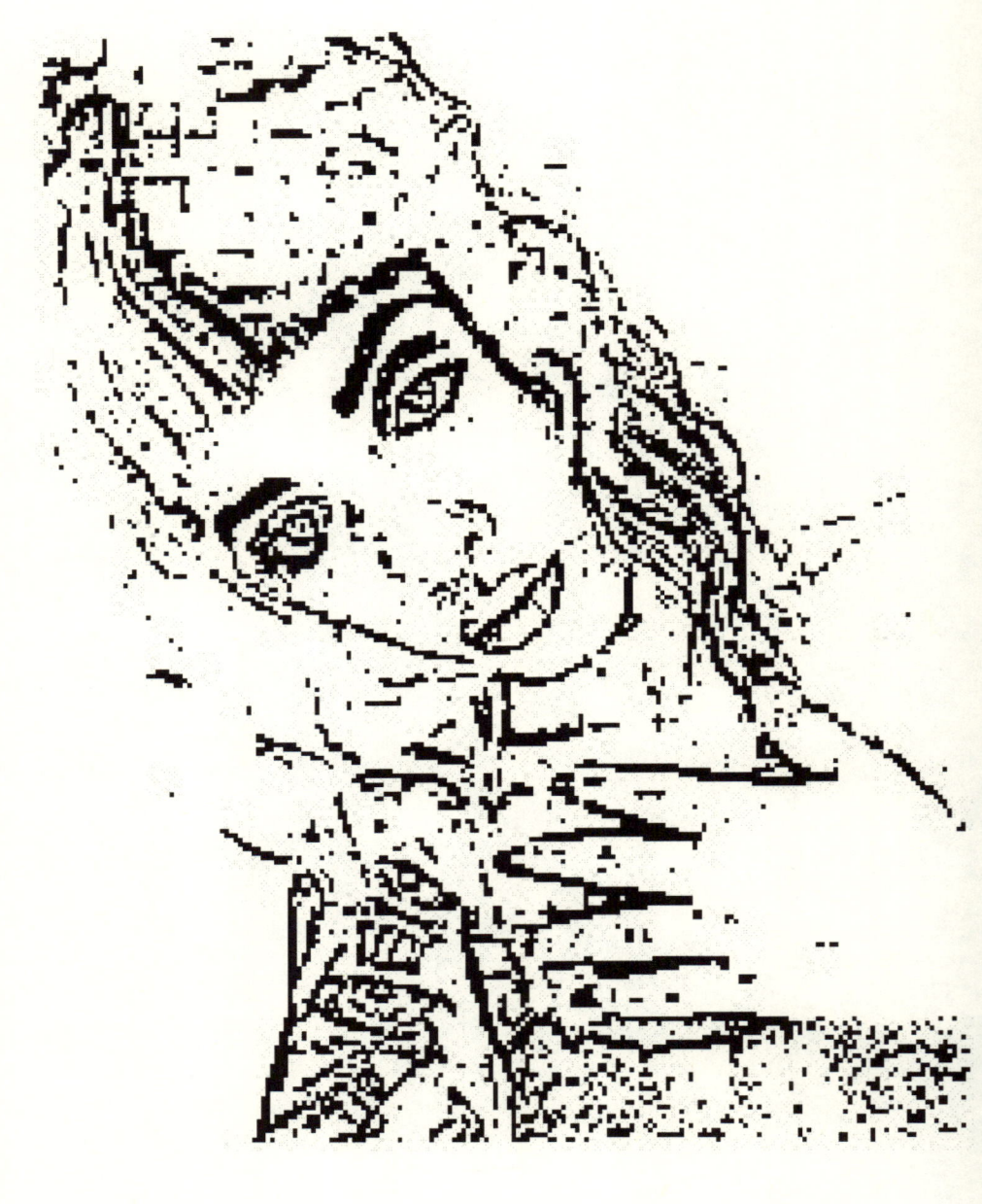

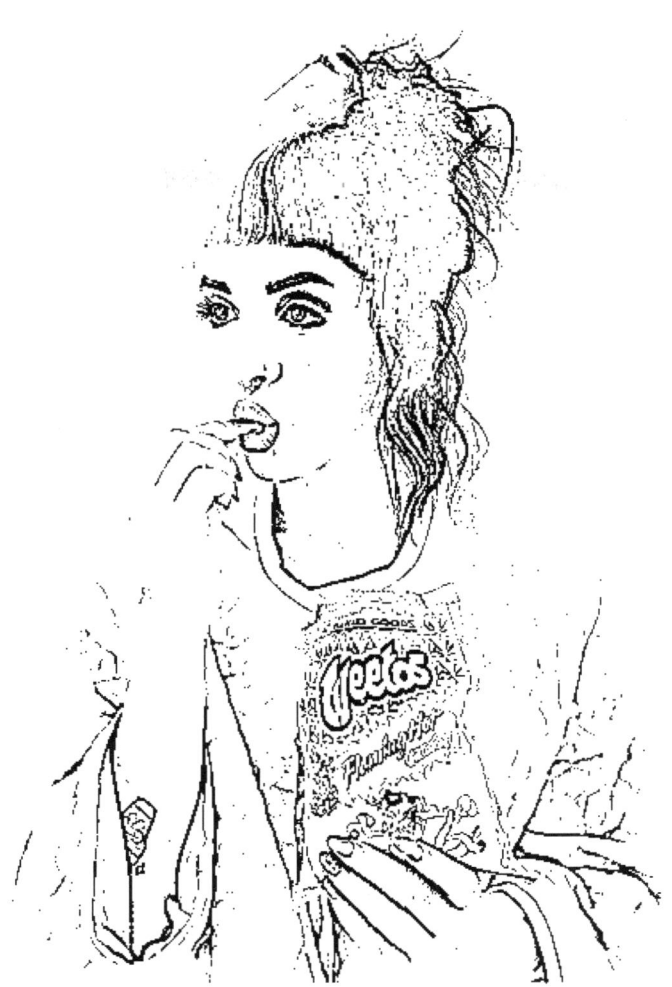

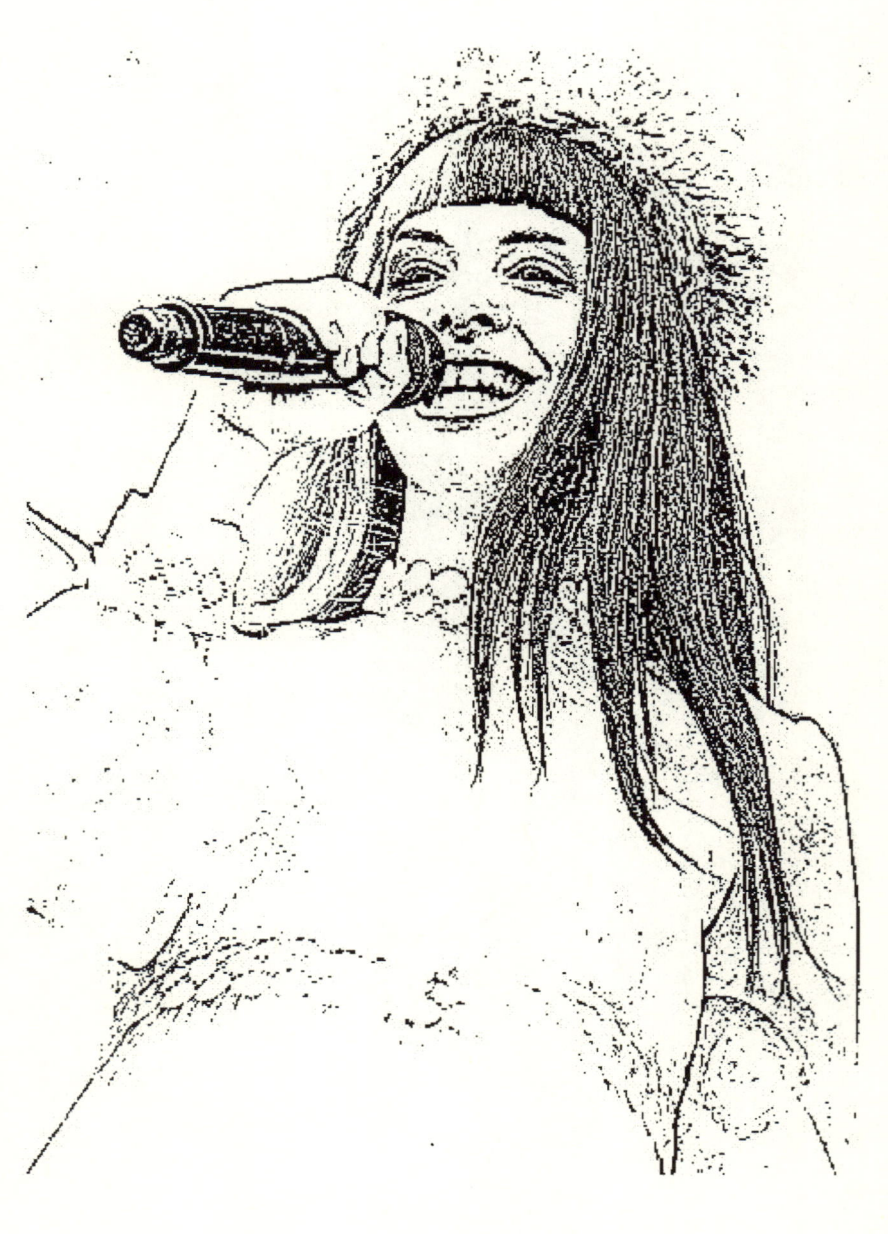

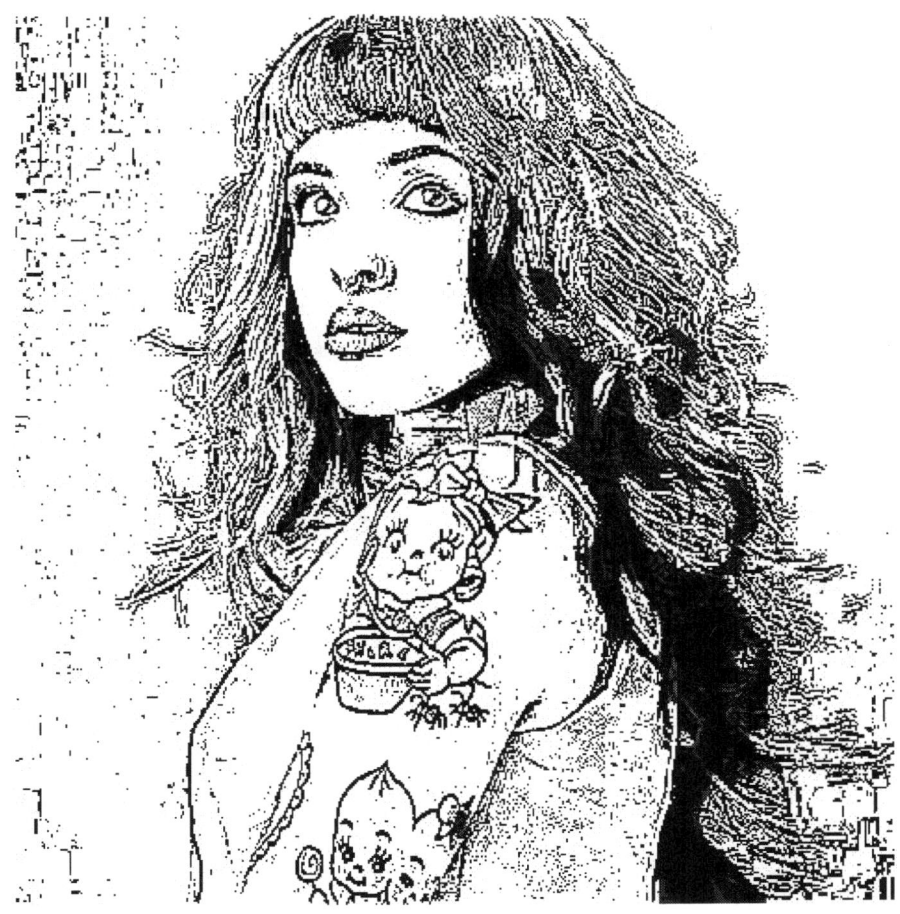

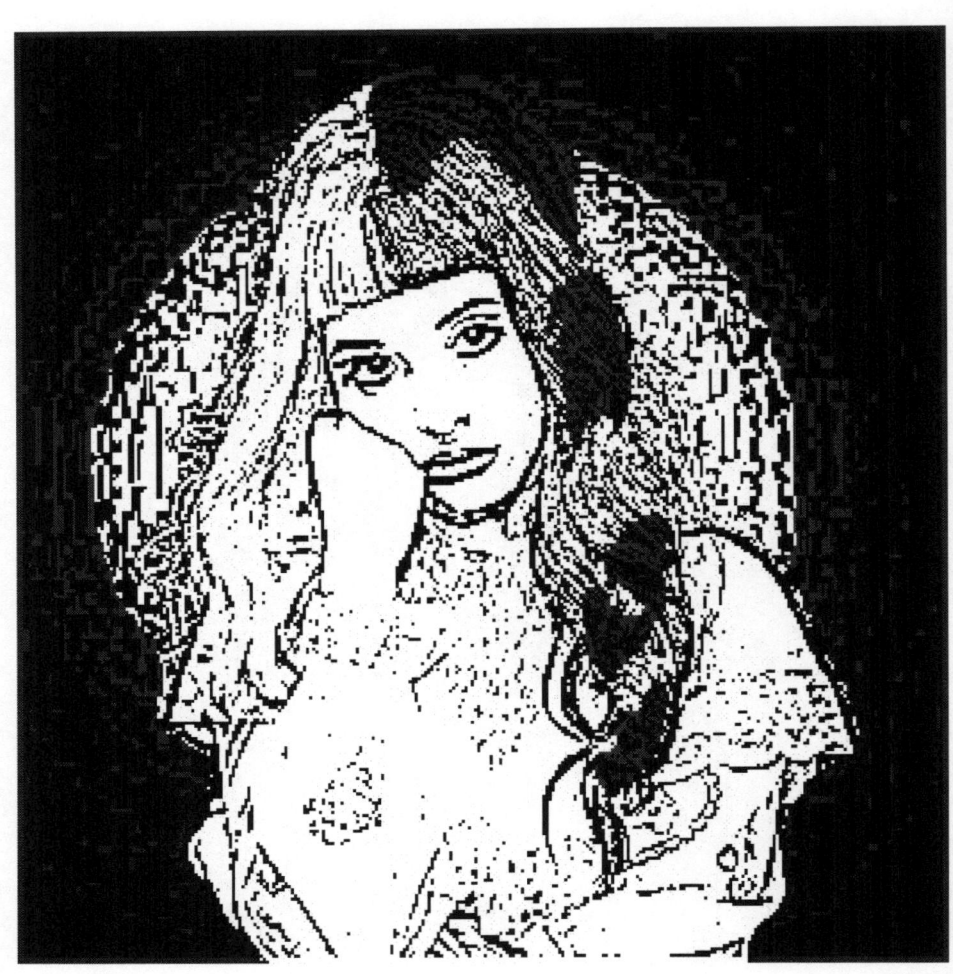

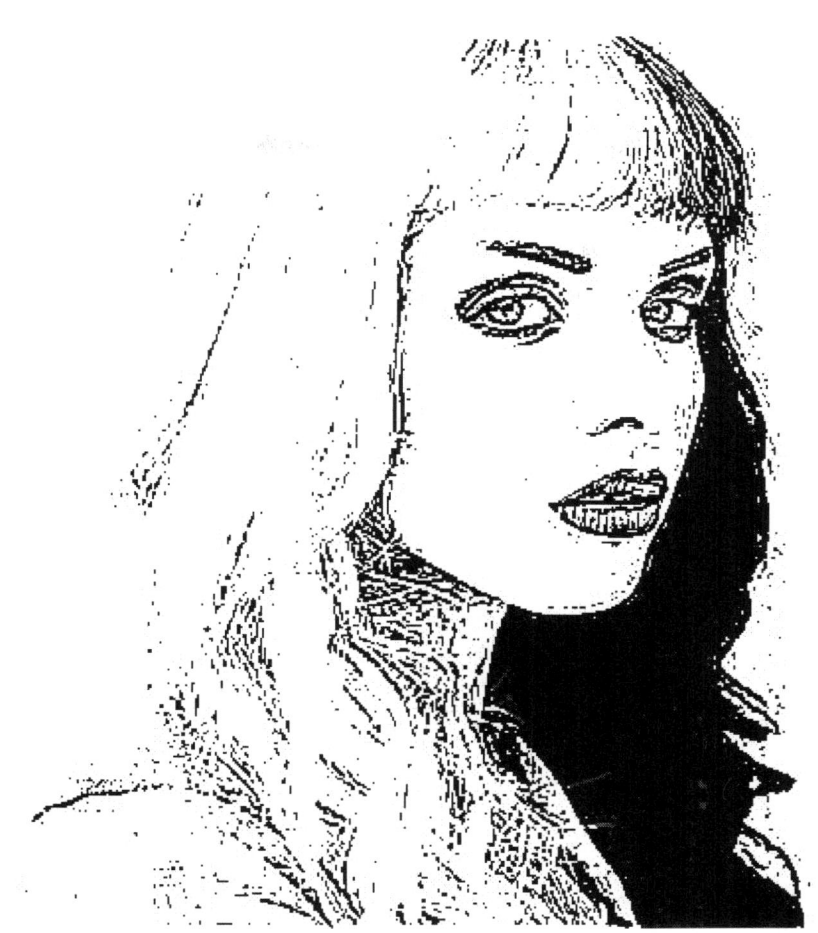

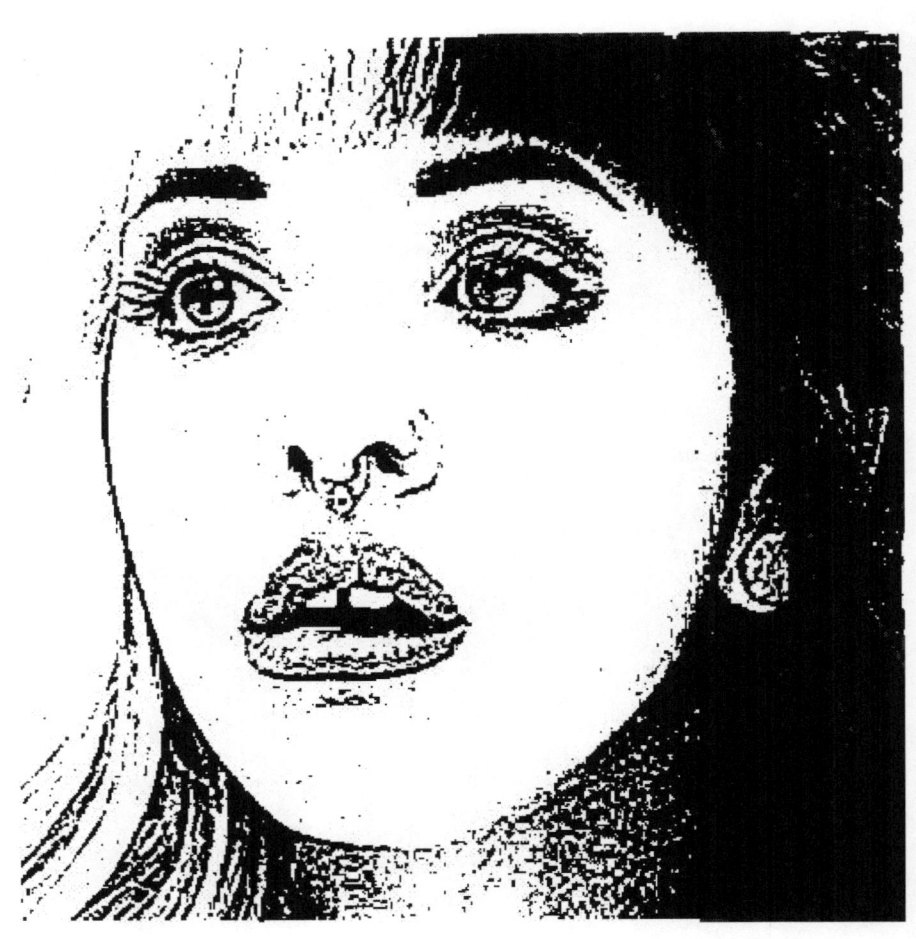

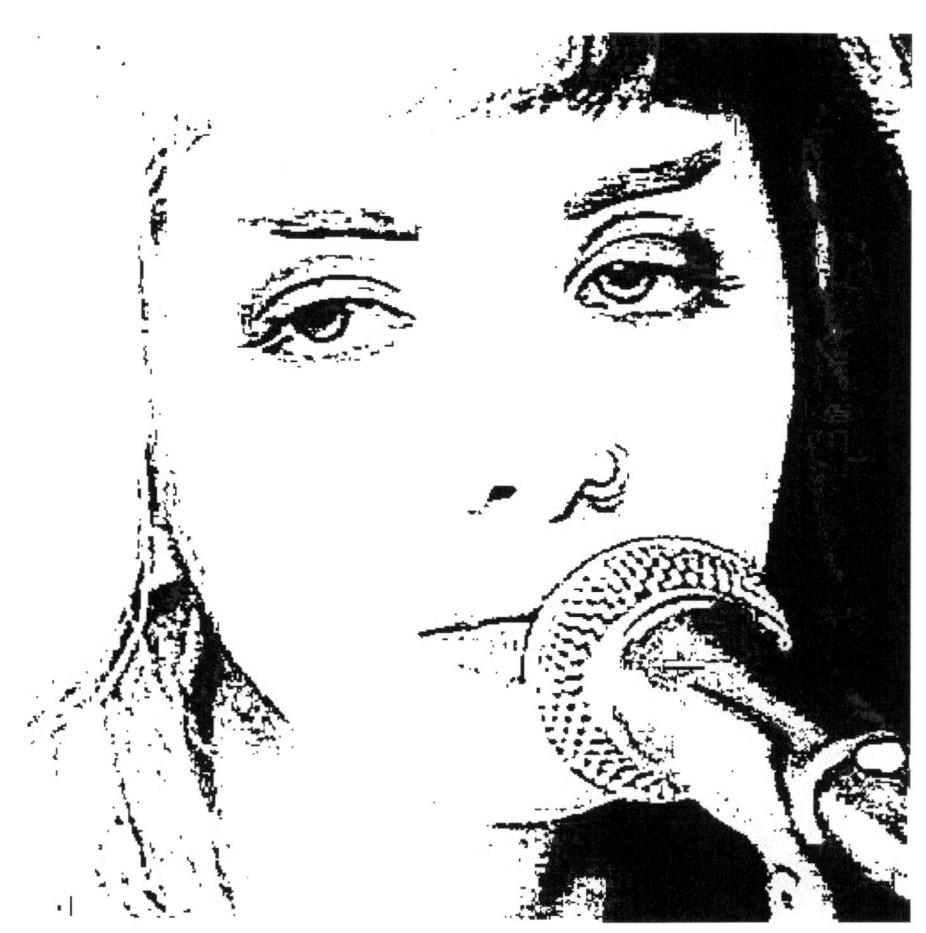

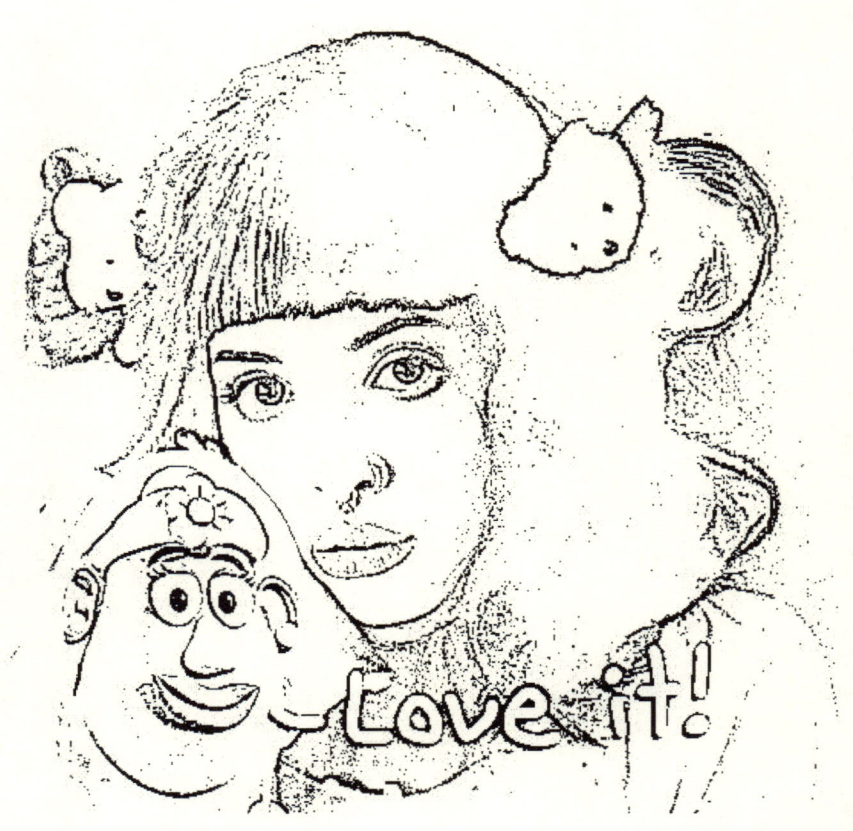

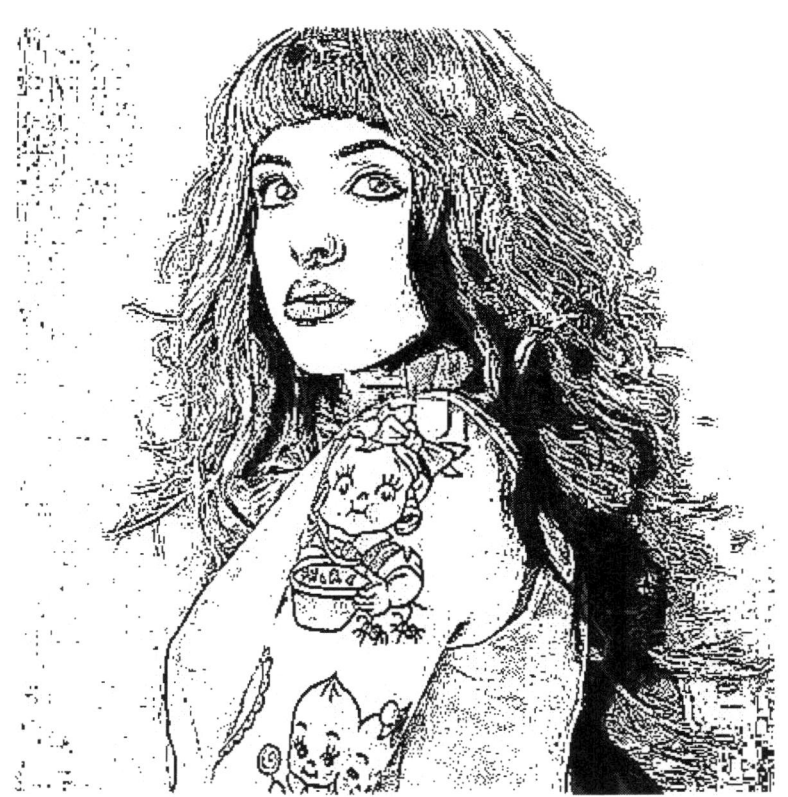

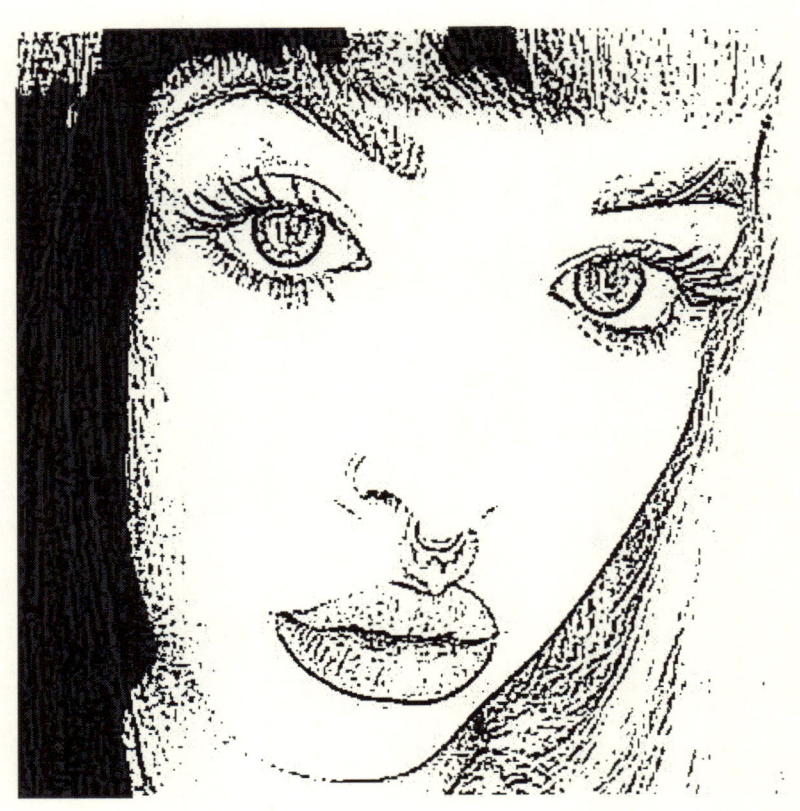

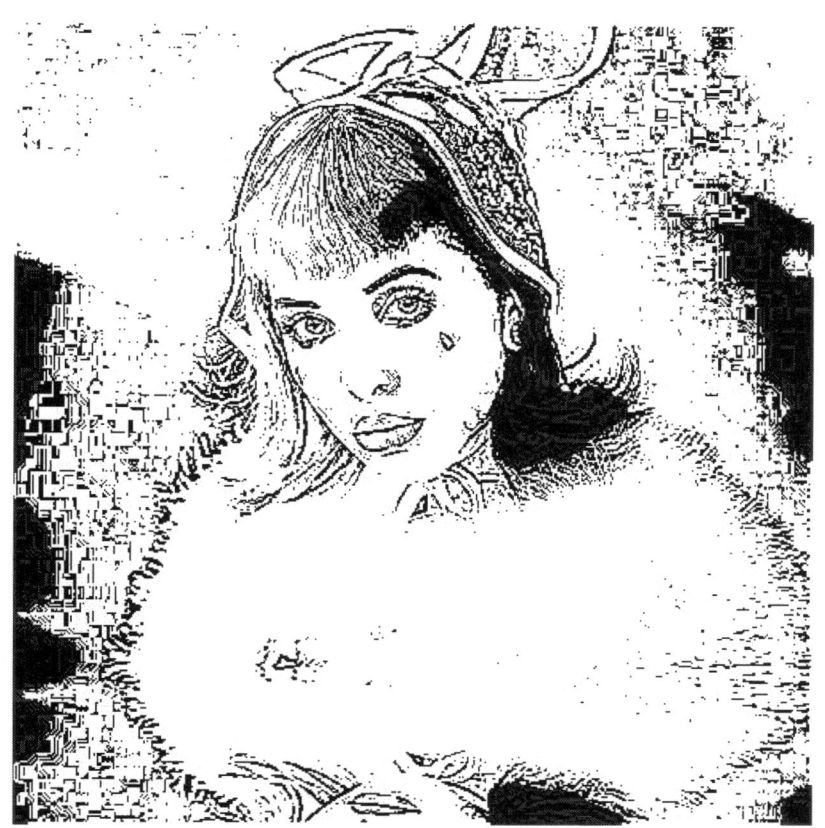

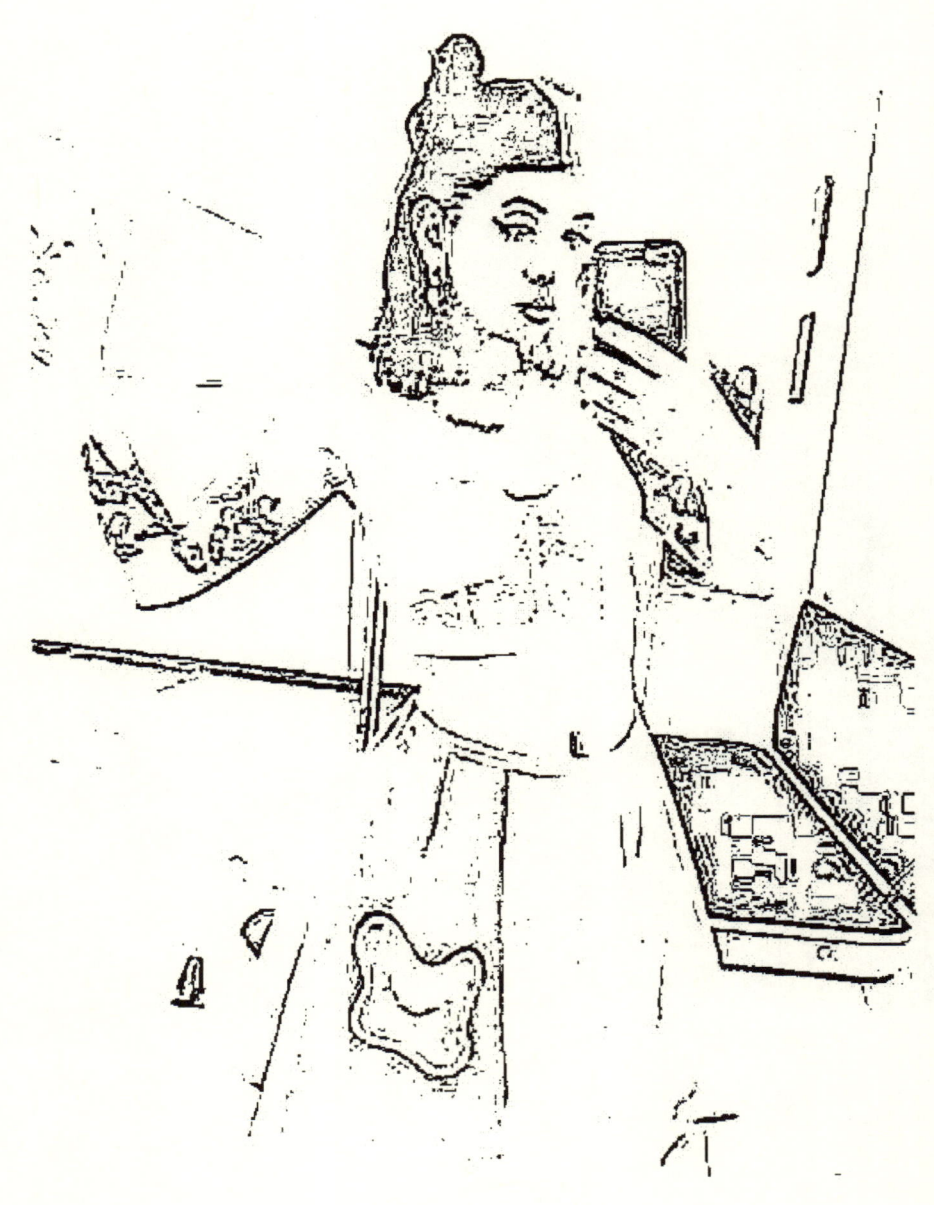

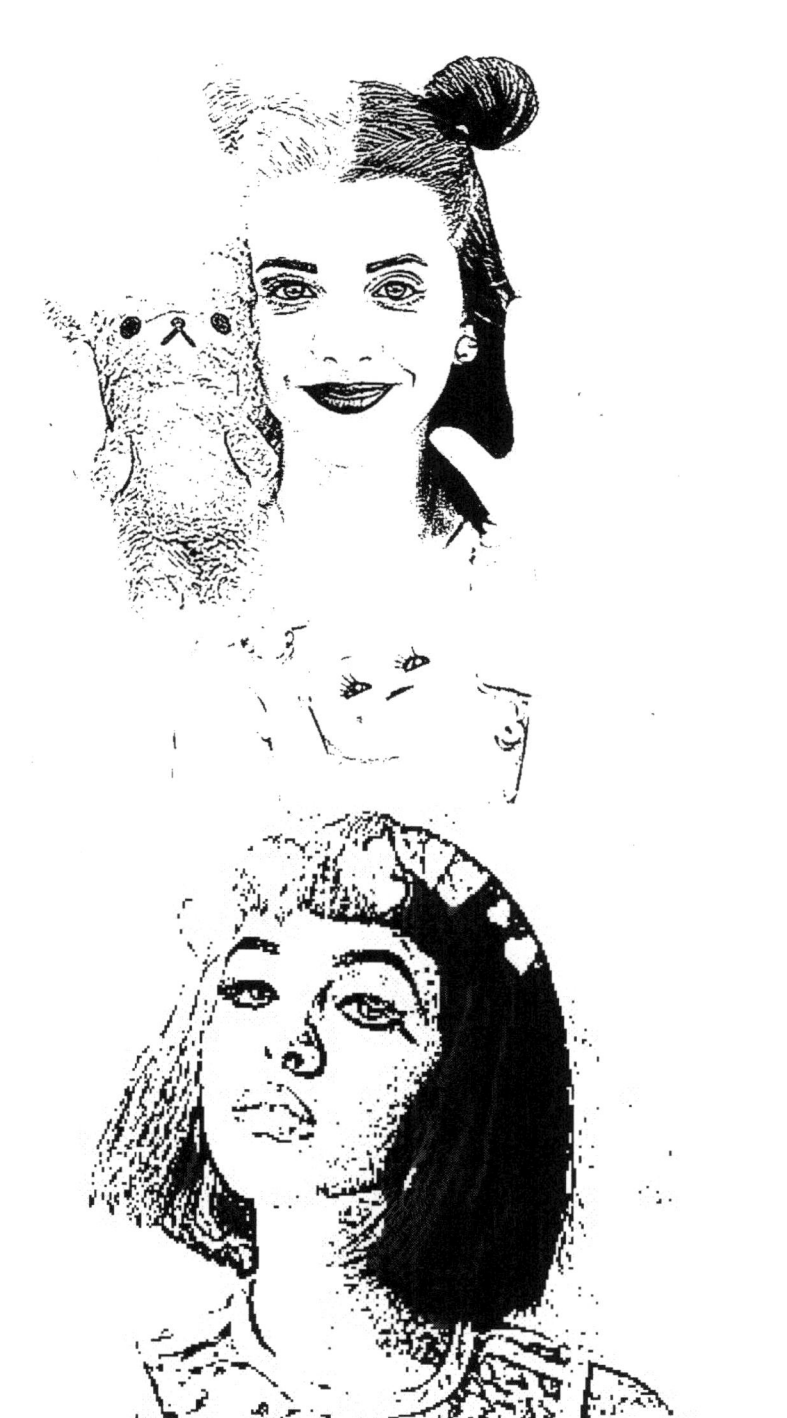

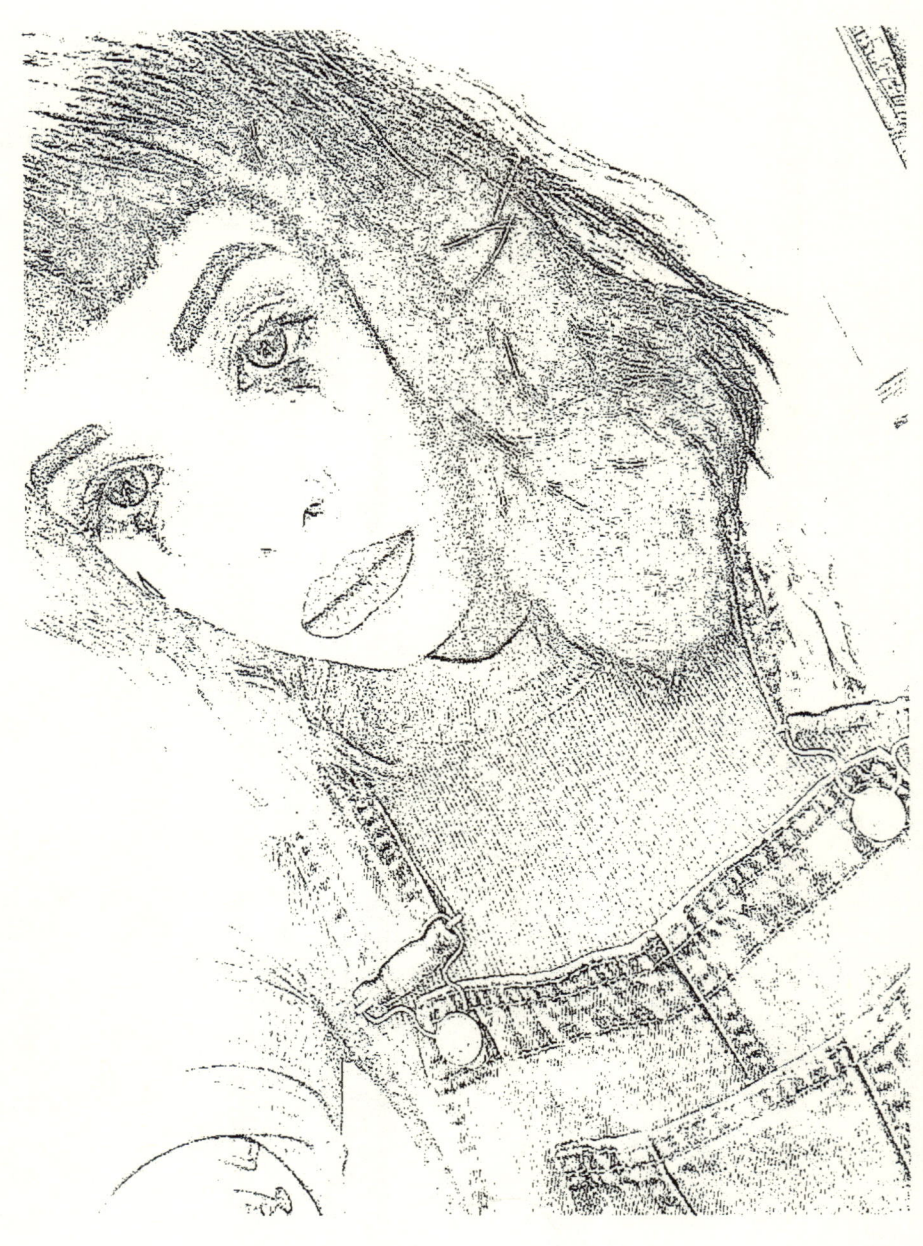

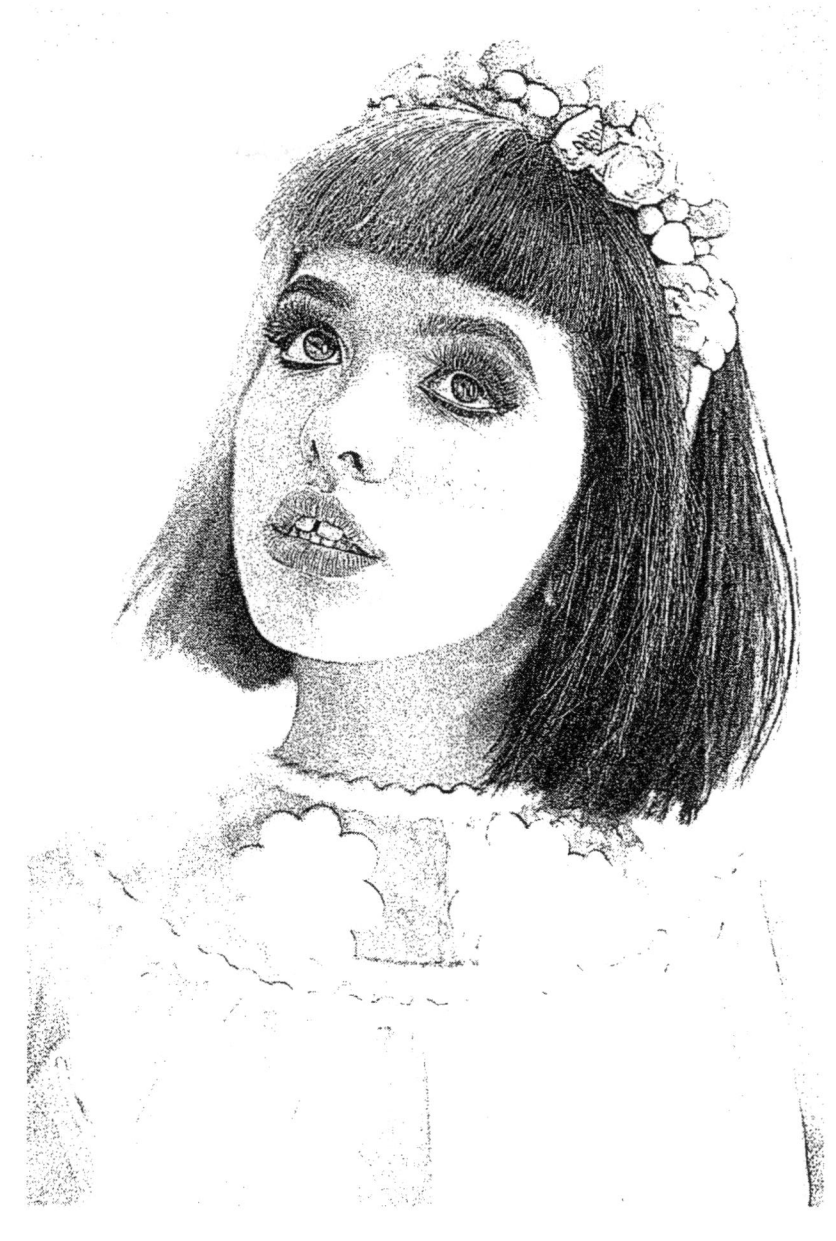

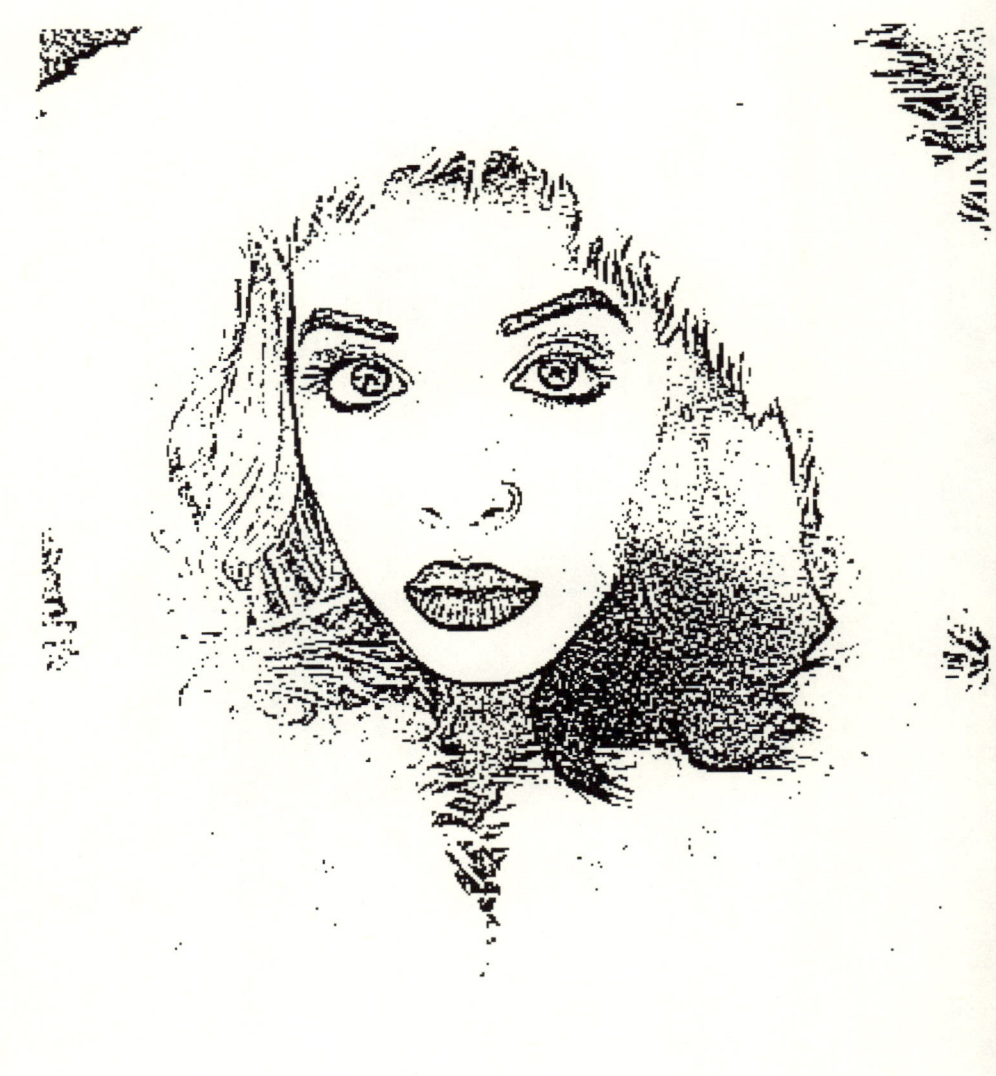

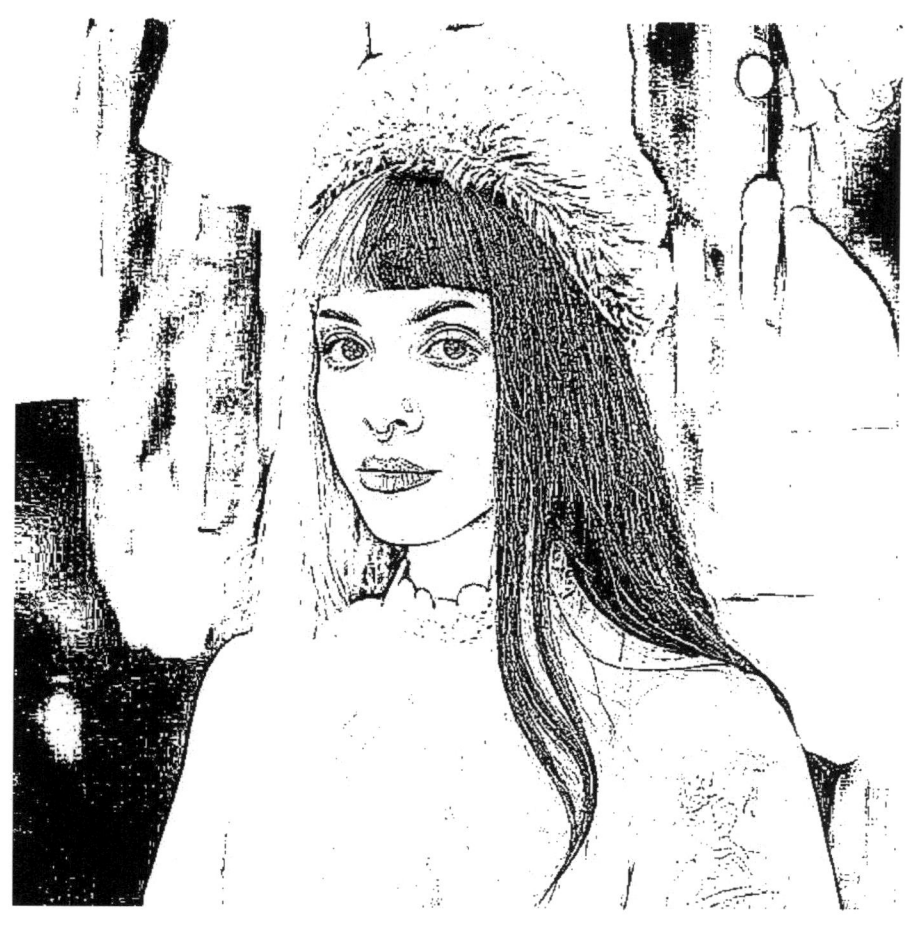

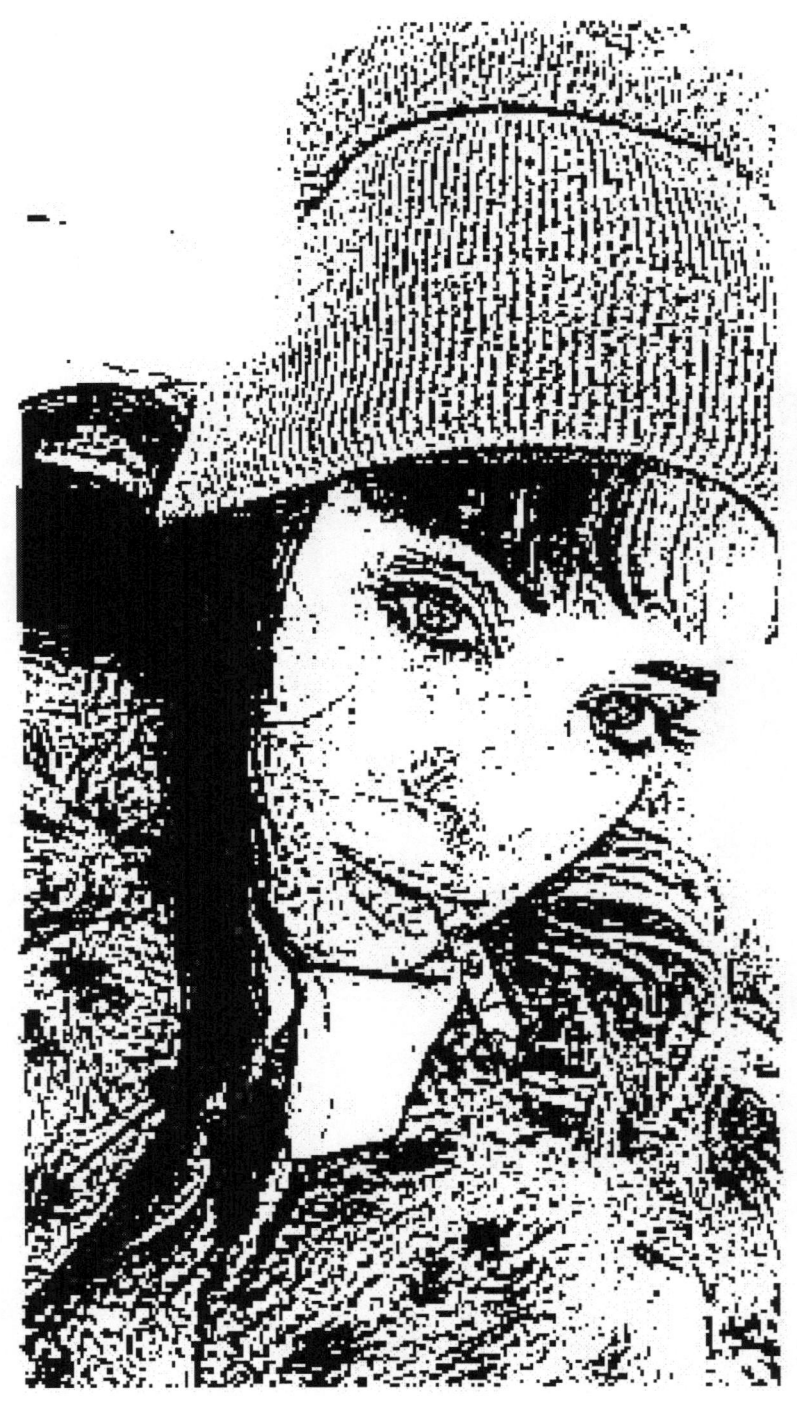

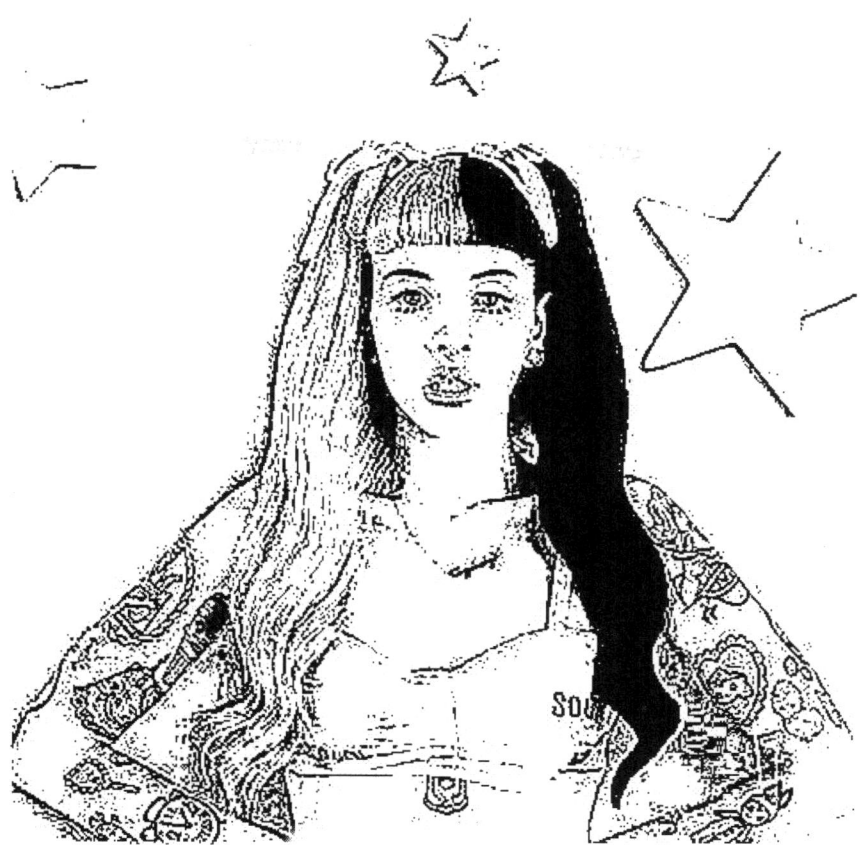

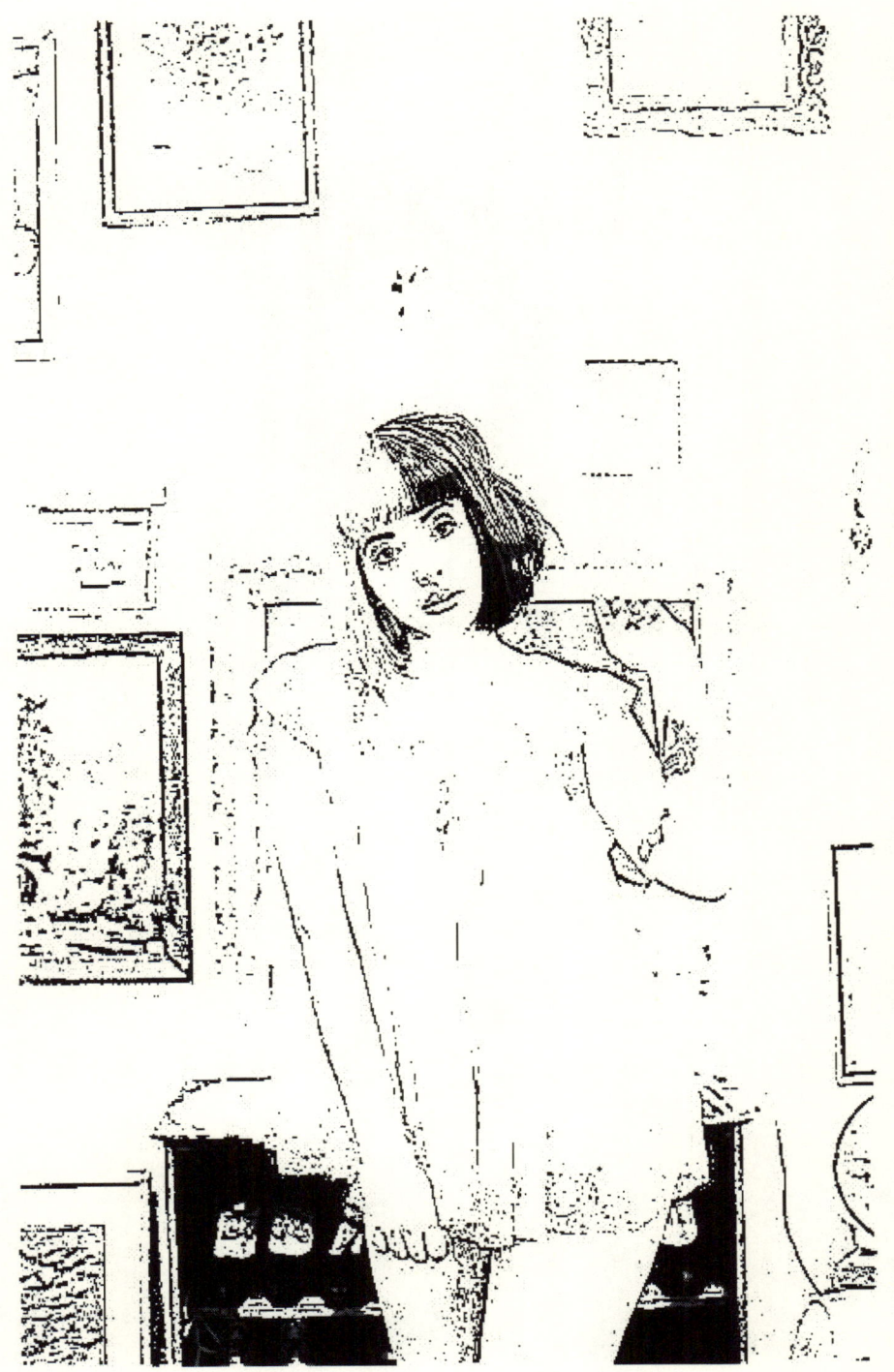

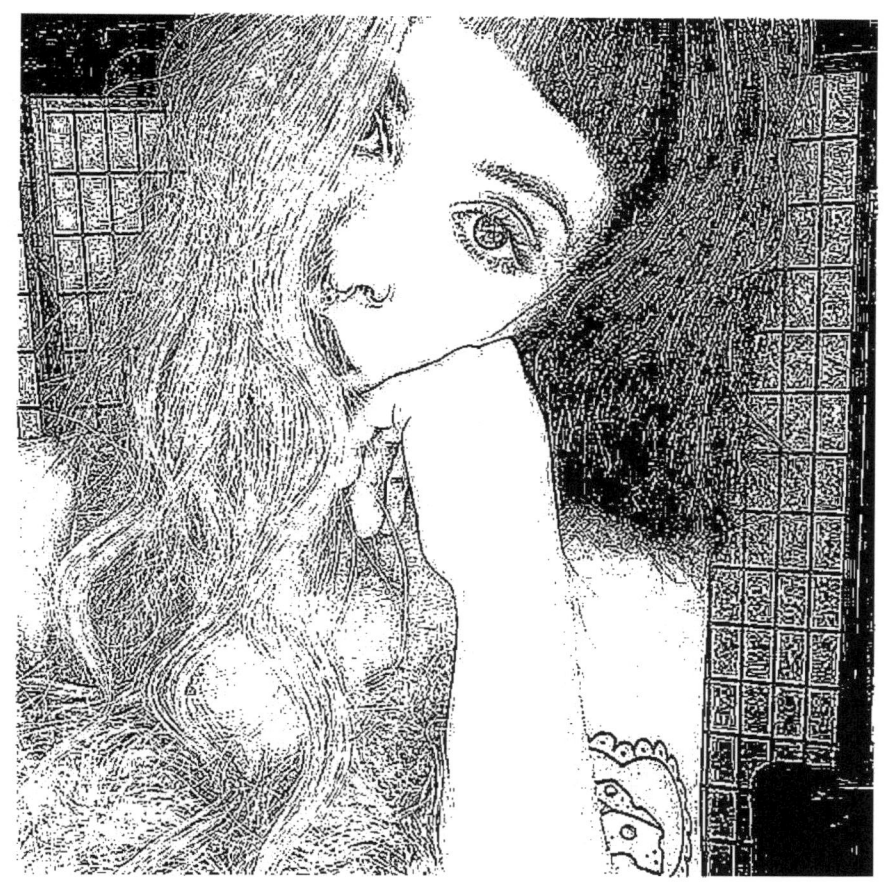

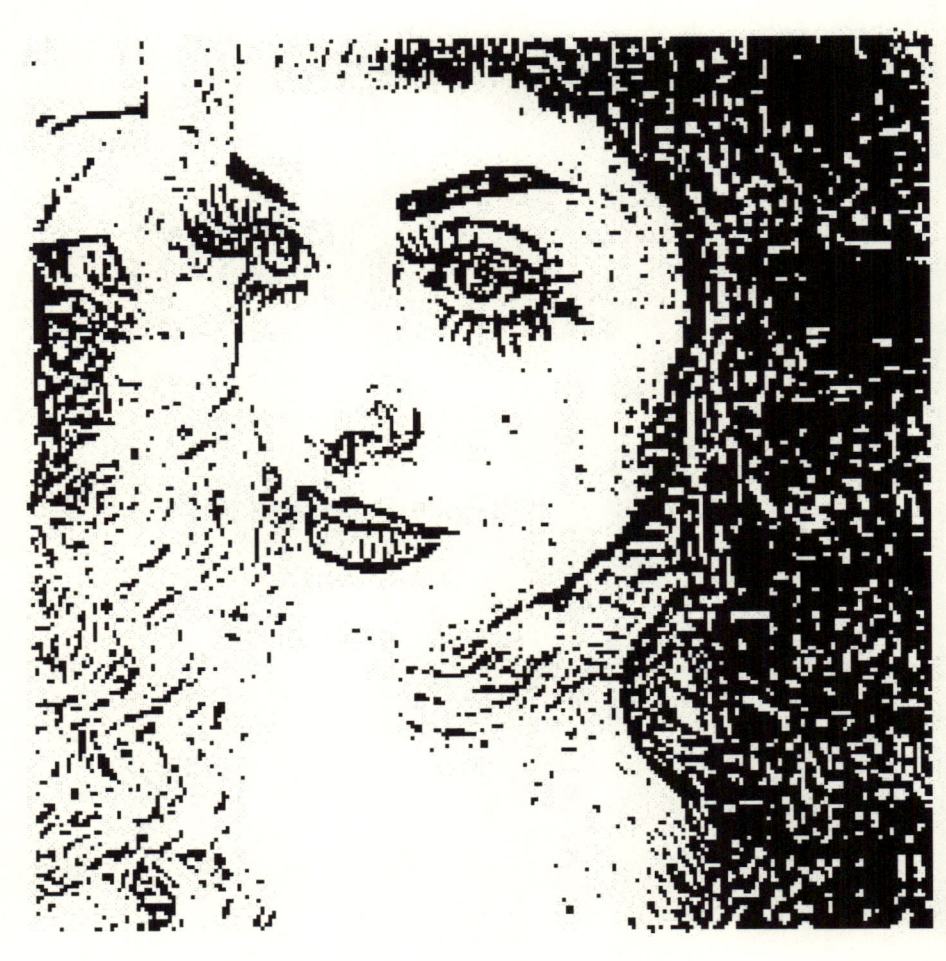

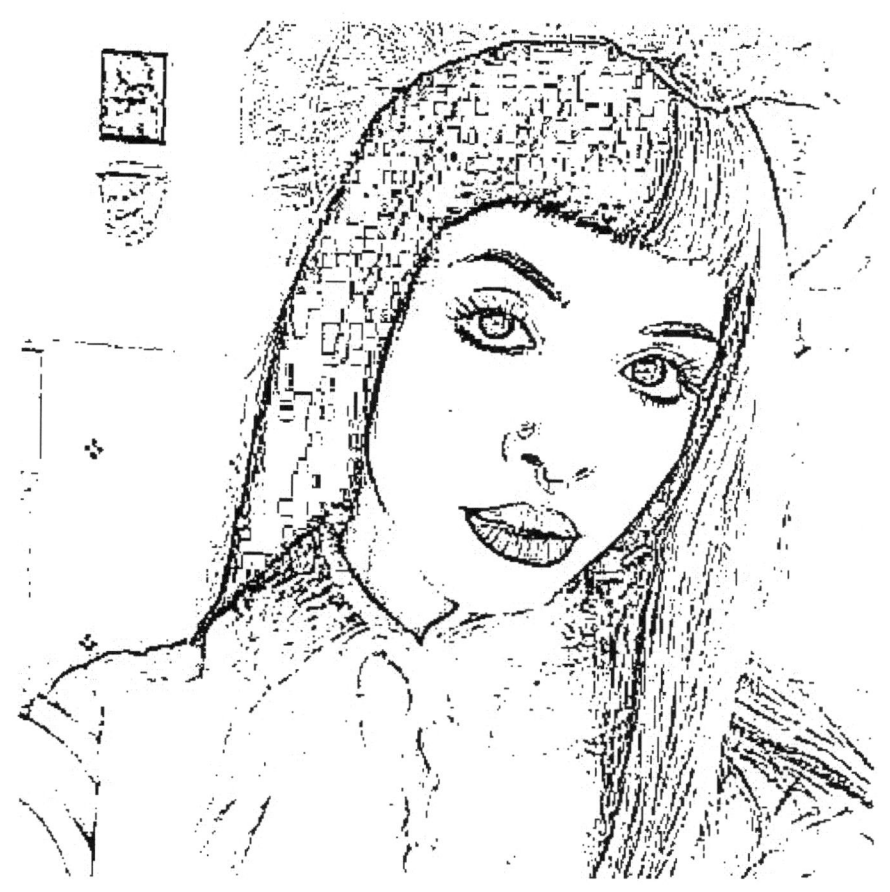

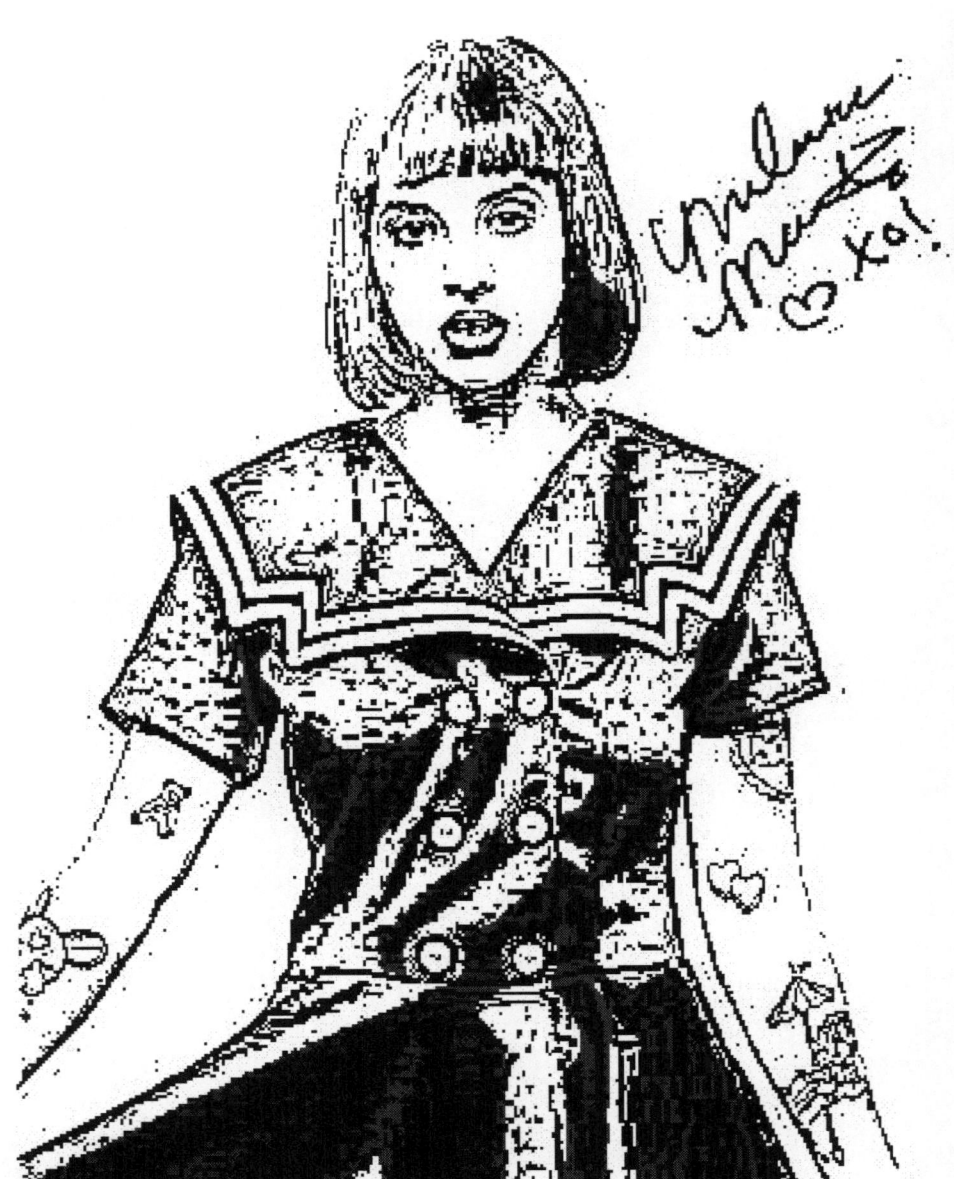

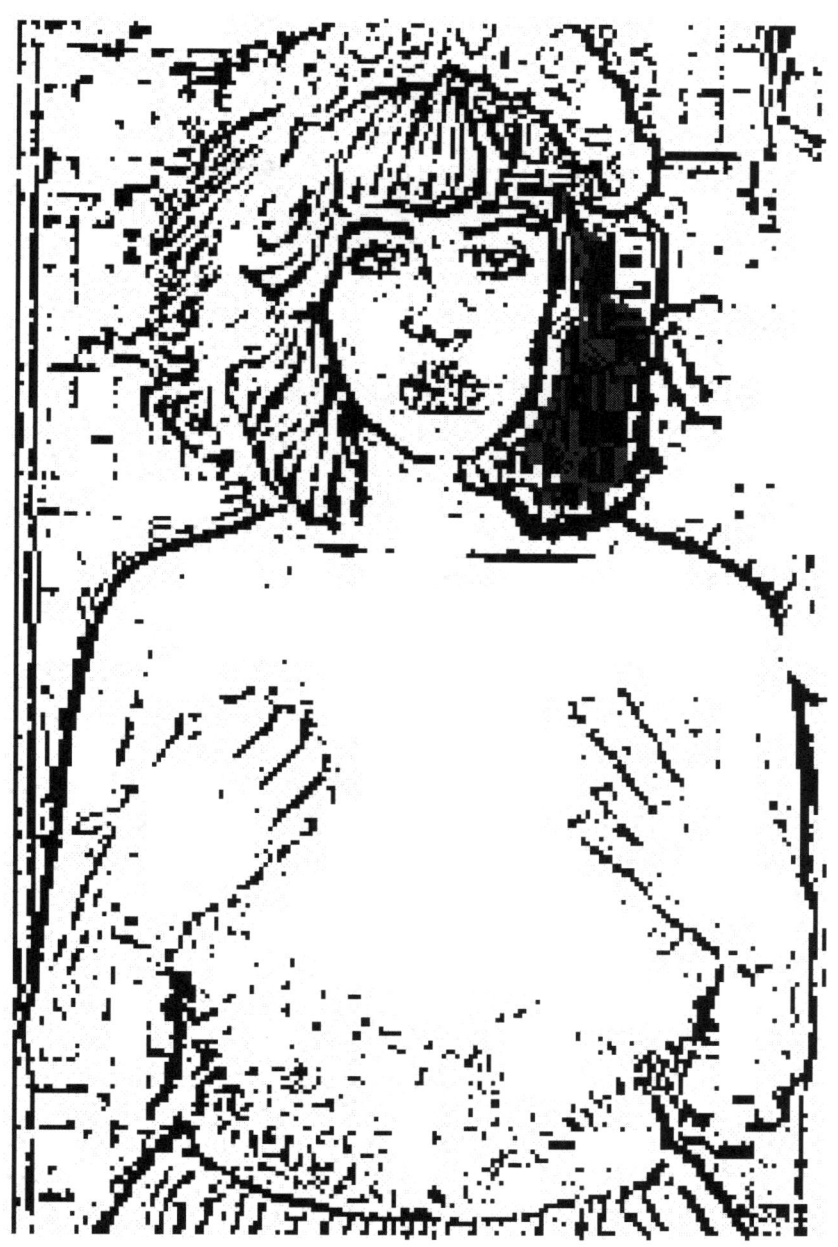

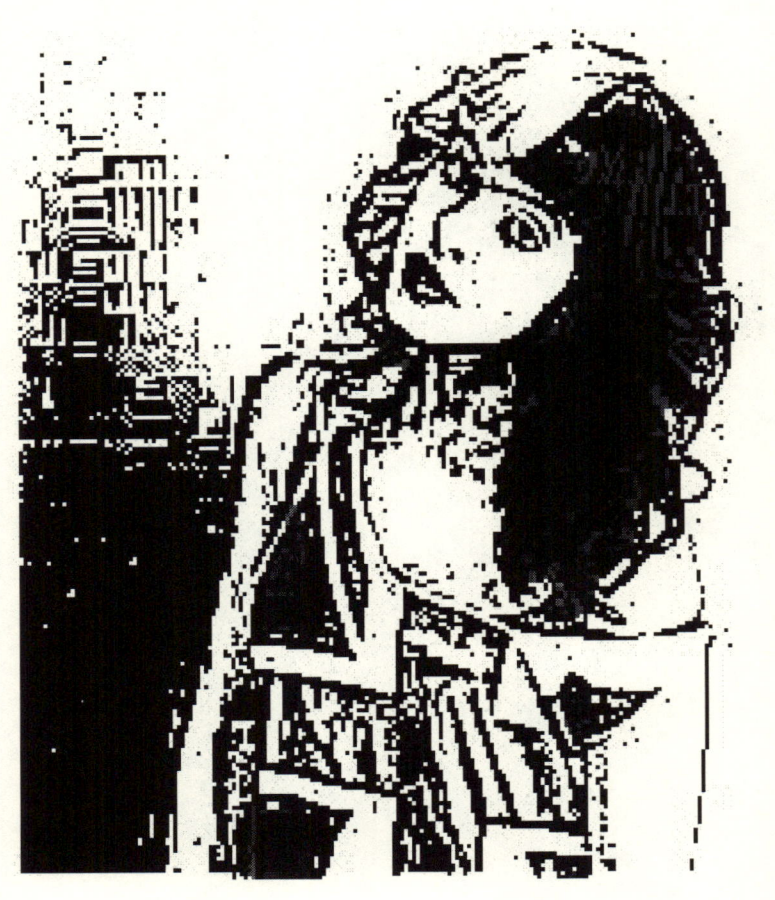

Made in the USA
Monee, IL
01 December 2019

17715113R00021